Getting in Shape

for Bass

by Cassia Harvey

edited by Matthew Roberts

CHP126

©2004 by C. Harvey Publications All Rights Reserved.

www.charveypublications.com - print books
www.learnstrings.com - PDF downloadable books
www.harveystringarrangements.com - chamber music

Less-advanced (A) pages are structured so that they can be played together with more-advanced (B) pages.

Contents

Page		Page	
2	Finger Trainer (A)	30	Exercise for Both Hands (A/B)
3	Little Brown Jug (A)	31	Karobushka (A/B)
4	Finger Trainer (B)	32	Pre-Skipping (A)
5	Little Brown Jug (B)	33	Fireworks Music (A)
6	Finger Workout (A)	34	Pre-Skipping (B)
7	Soldier's Chorus (A)	35	Fireworks Music (B)
8	Finger Workout (B)	36	Skipping (A)
9	Soldier's Chorus (B)	37	Arkansas Traveler (A)
10	Daily Exercise (A)	38	Skipping (B)
11	The Frog Went A-Courting (A)	39	Arkansas Traveler (B)
12	Daily Exercise (B)	40	First Position Workout (A)
13	The Frog Went A-Courting (B)	41	High Cap (A)
14	Finger & Bow Workout (A)	42	First Position Workout (B)
15	Turkish Dance (A)	43	High Cap (B)
16	Finger & Bow Workout (B)	44	Pre-Skipping (A)
17	Turkish Dance (B)	45	Pickles for Breakfast (A)
18	Pre-Skipping (A)	46	Pre-Skipping (B)
19	Hopak (A)	47	Pickles for Breakfast (B)
20	Pre-Skipping (B)	48	Skipping (A)
21	Hopak (B)	49	Chicken on the Fence Post (A)
22	Skipping (A)	50	Skipping (B)
23	Brandenburg 5 (A)	51	Chicken on the Fence Post (B)
24	Skipping (B)	52	First Position Workout (A)
25	Brandenburg 5 (B)	53	Flower Song (A)
26	Strength Exercise (A)	54	First Position Workout (B)
27	Mairi's Wedding (A)	55	Flower Song (B)
28	Strength Exercise (B)	56	Skipping (A)
29	Mairi's Wedding (B)	57	The British Grenadiers (A)
		58	Skipping (B)
		59	The British Grenadiers (B)

Getting in Shape for Bass

Finger Trainer (A)

Edited by Matthew Roberts

Cassia Harvey

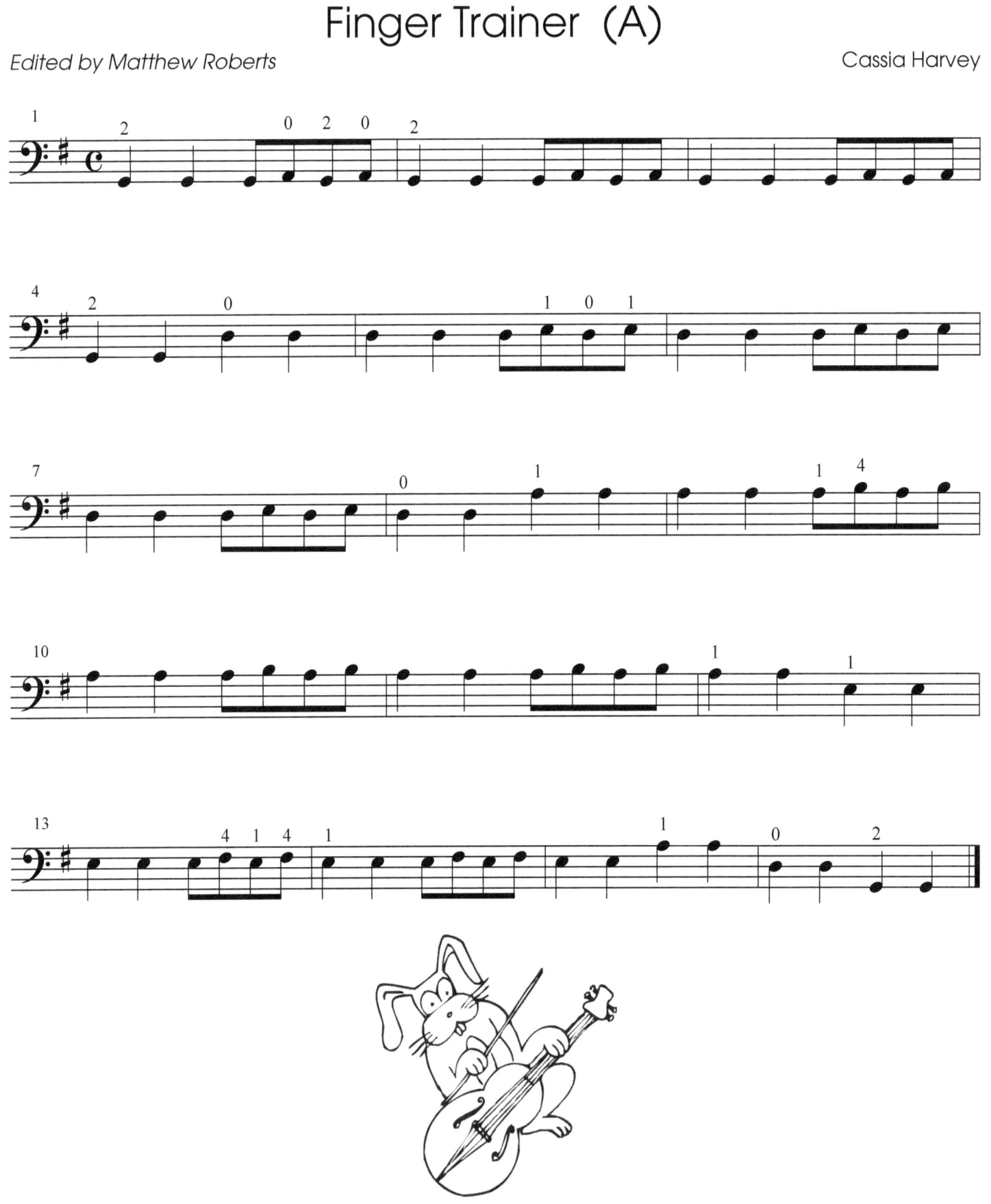

©2005 C. Harvey Publications All Rights Reserved.

Little Brown Jug (A)

Trad./arr. C. Harvey

©2005 C. Harvey Publications All Rights Reserved.

Finger Trainer (B)

Cassia Harvey

Getting in Shape for Bass

Little Brown Jug (B)

Trad./arr. C. Harvey

Second Position

Second Position

Finger Workout (A)

Cassia Harvey

©2005 C. Harvey Publications All Rights Reserved.

Soldier's Chorus (A)

Bizet/arr. C. Harvey

Finger Workout (B)

Cassia Harvey

Soldier's Chorus (B)

Bizet/arr. C. Harvey

Daily Exercise (A)

Cassia Harvey

The Frog Went A-Courting (A)

Trad./arr. C. Harvey

Getting in Shape for Bass

The Frog Went A-Courting (B)
Trad./arr. C. Harvey

©2005 C. Harvey Publications All Rights Reserved.

Finger and Bow Workout (A)

Cassia Harvey

©2005 C. Harvey Publications All Rights Reserved.

Turkish Dance (A)

Kruckow/arr. C. Harvey

Finger and Bow Workout (B)

Cassia Harvey

Turkish Dance (B)

Kruckow/arr. C. Harvey

©2005 C. Harvey Publications All Rights Reserved.

Pre-Skipping (A)

Cassia Harvey

Hopak (A)

Mussorgsky/arr. C. Harvey

Pre-Skipping (B)

Cassia Harvey

Getting in Shape for Bass

Hopak (B)

Mussorgsky/arr. C. Harvey

Brandenburg 5 (A)

Bach/arr. C. Harvey

Skipping (B)

Cassia Harvey

Getting in Shape for Bass

Brandenburg 5 (B)

Bach/arr. C. Harvey

©2005 C. Harvey Publications All Rights Reserved.

Strength Exercise (A)

Cassia Harvey

©2005 C. Harvey Publications All Rights Reserved.

Mairi's Wedding (A)

Trad./arr. C. Harvey

Mairi's Wedding (B)

Trad./arr. C. Harvey

Karobushka (A/B)

Trad./arr. C. Harvey

Pre-Skipping (A)

Cassia Harvey

Fireworks Music (A)

Handel/arr. C. Harvey

Pre-Skipping (B)

Cassia Harvey

Fireworks Music (B)

Handel/arr. C. Harvey

Skipping (A)

Cassia Harvey

Arkansas Traveler (A)

Trad./arr. C. Harvey

Skipping (B)

Cassia Harvey

Arkansas Traveler (B)

Trad./arr. C. Harvey

First Position Workout (A)

Cassia Harvey

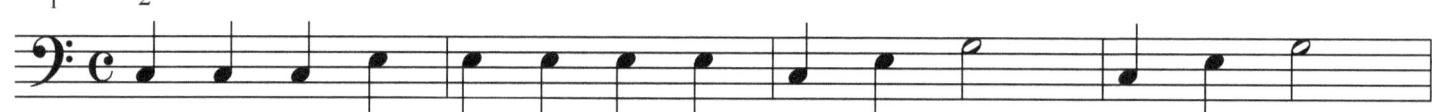

©2005 C. Harvey Publications All Rights Reserved.

High Cap (A)

Trad./arr. C. Harvey

First Position Workout (B)

Cassia Harvey

©2005 C. Harvey Publications All Rights Reserved.

High Cap (B)

Trad./arr. C. Harvey

Pre-Skipping (A)

Cassia Harvey

Pickles for Breakfast (A)

Trad./arr. C. Harvey

Pre-Skipping (B)

Cassia Harvey

Pickles for Breakfast (B)

Trad./arr. C. Harvey

Skipping (A)

Cassia Harvey

Getting in Shape for Bass

Chicken on the Fence Post (A)

Trad./arr. C. Harvey

©2005 C. Harvey Publications All Rights Reserved.

Chicken on the Fence Post (B)

Trad./arr. C. Harvey

First Position Workout (A)

Cassia Harvey

Flower Song (A)

Trad./arr. C. Harvey

First Position Workout (B)

Cassia Harvey

Flower Song (B)

Trad./arr. C. Harvey

Skipping (A)

Cassia Harvey

The British Grenadiers (A)

Trad./arr. C. Harvey

The British Grenadiers (B)

Getting in Shape for Bass

Trad./arr. C. Harvey

Available from www.charveypublications.com
Sailing Into Bethlehem: Compatible Christmas Duets for Strings

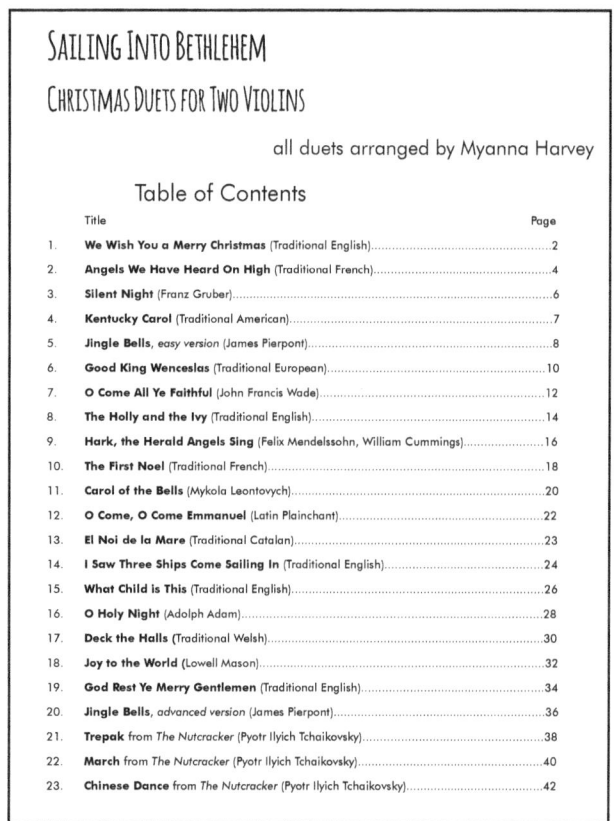

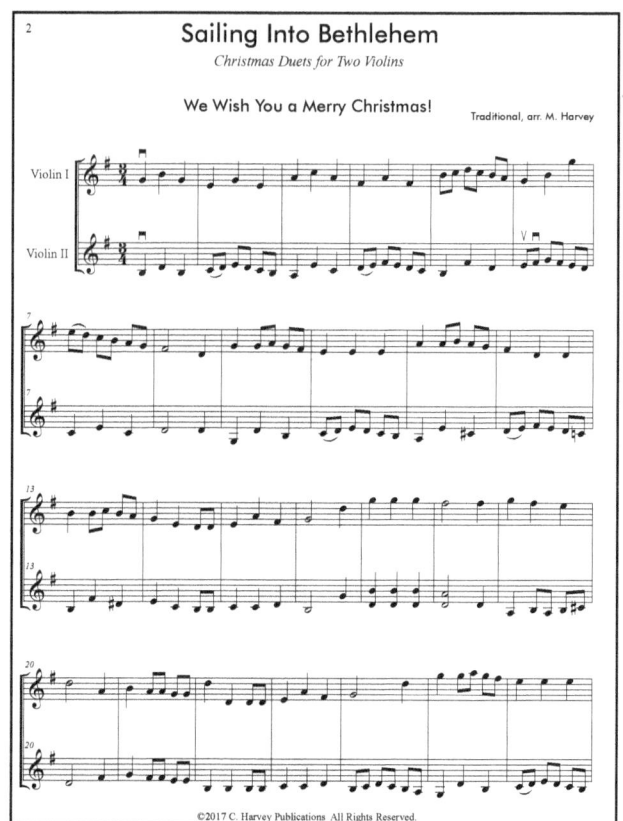

CHP333

CHP334

CHP335